Once Upon Ice

And Other Frozen Poems

Selected by *Jane Yolen*

Photographs by *Jason Stemple*

Wordsong / Boyds Mills Press

Published by Wordsong
Boyds Mills Press, Inc.
A Highlights Company
815 Church Street
Honesdale, Pennsylvania 18431
Printed in China

Publisher Cataloging-in-Publication Data (U.S.)

Yolen, Jane.
Once upon ice: and other frozen poems | selected by Jane Yolen ;
photographs by Jason Stemple.—1st ed.
[48] p. : ill. ; cm.
Includes index.
Summary: Inspired by photographs of ice in primarily natural
forms, writers Jane Yolen, X.J. Kennedy, Lee Bennett Hopkins,
and others capture their thoughts in poetry.
ISBN 1-56397-408-8 hc • ISBN 1-59078-174-0 pb
1. Ice—Juvenile Poetry. 2. Children's Poetry—Collections.
[1. Ice—Poetry. 2. Poetry—Collections.] I. Yolen, Jane.
II. Stemple, Jason, ill. III. Title.
811.008—dc20 1997 AC CIP
Library of Congress Catalog Card Number 96-84165

First Boyds Mills Press paperback edition, 2003
First edition, 1997
Book designed by Joy Chu
The text of this book is set in 18-point Simoncini Garamond.

Visit our Web site at www.boydsmillspress.com

10 9 8 7 6 5 4 hc   10 9 8 7 6 5 4 3 2 1 pb

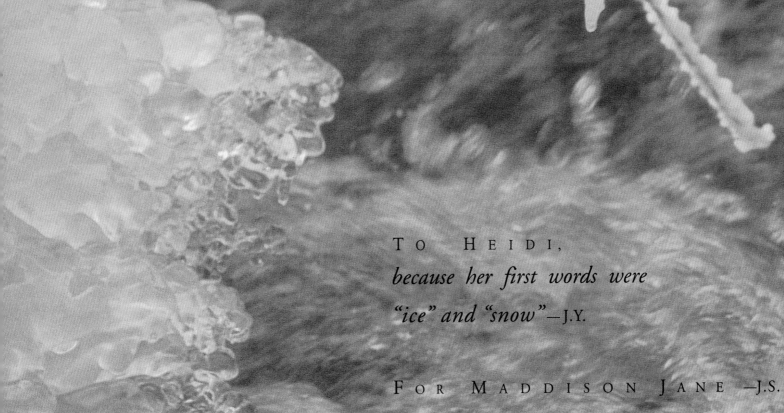

Contents

A Note from the Editor   [6]

Ice Can Scream   *Jane Yolen*   [8]

The Opera of the Ice   *Marvin Bell*   [11]

Necklace   *Jane Yolen*   [12]

Chewing on Ice   *Kathi Appelt*   [13]

Autumn   *Ann Dixon*   [15]

Winter Wraps   *Carol E. Reed-Jones*   [16]

Dangerous Ice   *X.J. Kennedy*   [19]

Winter's Finger   *Carol Jane Bangs*   [20]

Pyramid   *Shulamith Levey Oppenheim*   [21]

Ice Cycle   *Mary Ann Hoberman*   [22]

My Dog, My Rough Champion   *J. Patrick Lewis*   [24]

Hieroglyph   *Ann Turner*   [25]

Cold Snap   *Bill Yake*   [26]

Once Upon Ice   *Christine Crow*   [27]

Icicles   *Lee Bennett Hopkins*   [29]

Ice Bridge   *Jane Yolen*   [30]

The Window in Winter   *Nancy Willard*   [32]

December Leaves   *J. Patrick Lewis*   [33]

Overnight Ice   *Barbara Davis*   [34]

Proteus   *Christine Crow*   [35]

Ice Sisters   *Pamela Powell*   [36]

Ice Cubes   *Jane Yolen*   [39]

A c k n o w l e d g m e n t s   [40]

A Note from the Editor

I asked a number of poets—some well known, some just beginning—to look at Jason Stemple's eerily wonderful photographs of ice formations and write whatever the photos inspired. Some reacted with rhyme, some created other poetic forms. Some saw specific pictures in the ice, others did not. Some wrote about how the photographs made them feel, and some guessed how the icy stuff might make someone else feel.

Now it is your turn—to read, to look at the images, and perhaps to write your *own* poems.

—*Jane Yolen*

Ice Can Scream

Ice can scream,
Ice can shout:
Winter in
And autumn out.

Ice can shout,
Ice can call,
Signaling
The end of fall.

Ice can call,
Ice can yell
Secrets no one
Else can tell.

Ice can yell,
Ice can howl,
Naming winter's
Weather foul.

Ice can howl,
Ice can wail,
Counting up
Each storm and gale.

Ice can wail,
Ice can shriek
Till the land
Is winter-bleak.

Ice can shriek,
Ice can scream
Straight across
The autumn dream.

Ice can scream,
Ice can shout:
Winter in
And autumn out.

—*Jane Yolen*

The Opera of the Ice

Once more, icy fingers
grip the creaking trees,
and ice crowds the leaves
from the drain spouts.
This year,
we'll have an ice flood,
ice boulders in the river,
mammoths that stalk spring—
to be set free.
And we will keep
even in spring
the memory of those warriors
who carried ice shields,
and white daggers
dripping with detachment.
We thought they would stay forever.
"I'll be going now," says ice,
"but I won't be far away.
Someday I'll slip into
your town again, OK?"

—*Marvin Bell*

Around its neck
The river wears
Jewels of ice—
Cabochon cut—
The flat side
Worn against the skin.
So I would wear
An ice necklace,
Had I the water-smooth shoulders
To display it,
Had I a taste for diamonds
And a capacity for cold.

—Jane Yolen

Necklace

Chewing on Ice

Here
Iceosaurs roam.
They dine on glacial calves
and play "King of the Iceberg."
Their favorite sport is
avalanching,
winner take all.
When they die,
they leave behind jagged teeth,
sharp reminders of their
terrible bites.

—*Kathi Appelt*

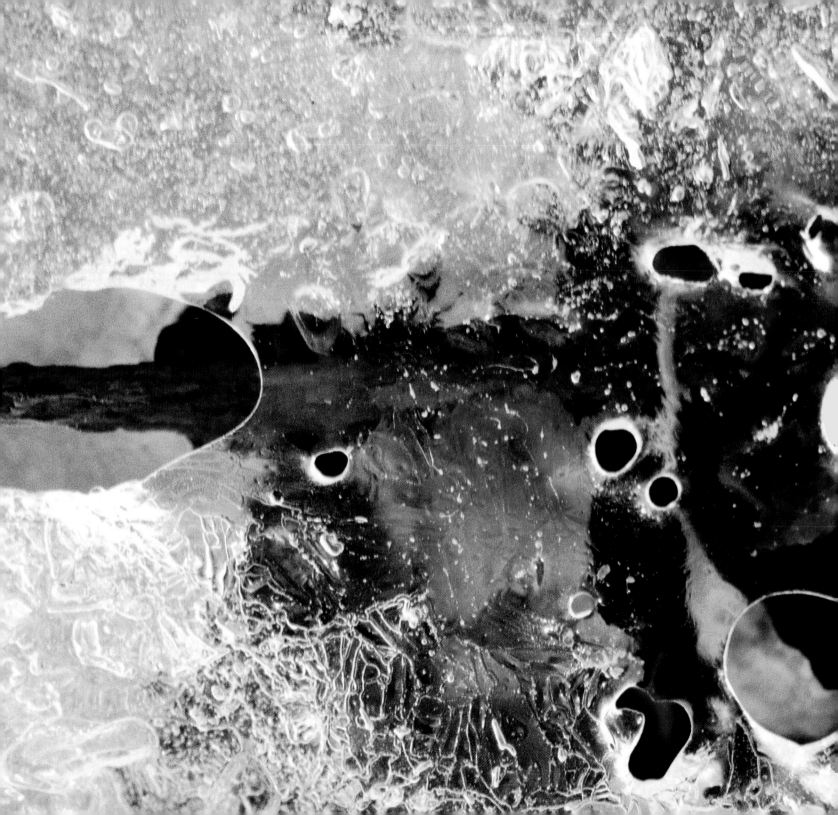

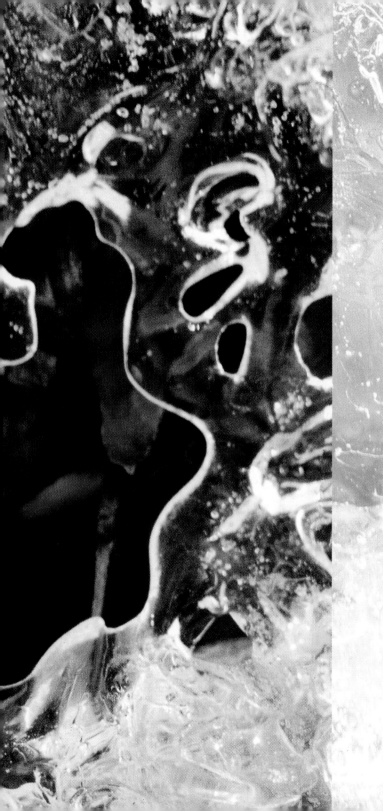

Autumn

Peeking through a curtain of cold,
Autumn leaves hide, tattered and old.
Yesterday's colors,
Yesterday's story
Dreaming already of next year's glory.

—*Ann Dixon*

Winter Wraps

Winter wraps
a brittle cape of cold
around a rock
and buttons it
with
a
single
leaf.

—*Carol E. Reed-Jones*

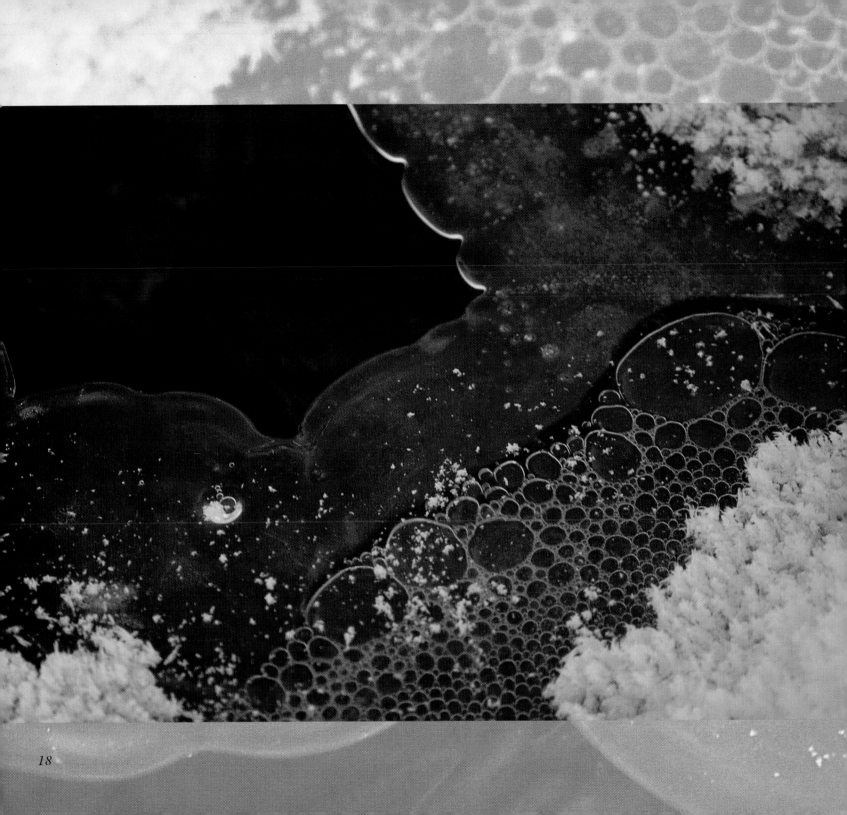

Dangerous Ice

Ice foams
Like sloshing suds,
But will it wash
People's duds?

Throw bubbling blue ice
In your washing machine
And your pet polar bear
Might come clean.

Or, chilly and chattering,
Tail turning blue,
He just might jump out,
Grab hold of you,

And with powerful paws,
Huge jaws that can crush,
Gulp you down like a cone
Of delicious slush.

So take my advice
And steer clear of trouble—
Run the opposite way
When you see ice bubble.

—X.J. Kennedy

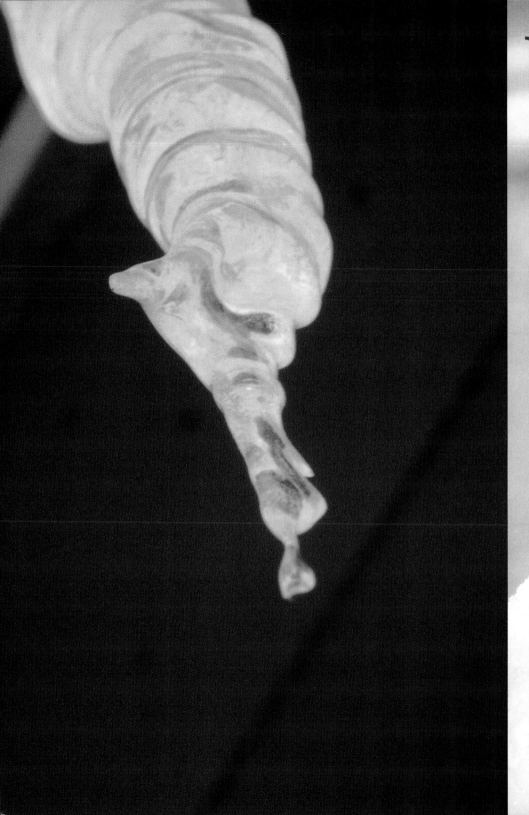

Winter's Finger

The old man holds out
one cold finger.
I try to see past
his frozen pointing,
try to imagine
what fear, what wonder
draws his attention
as the North Pole
draws the finger
of a compass.
Then I feel it:
ice in my bones—
something terrible
beckons to me.

—*Carol Jane Bangs*

Pyramid

Who dares scale you?
The cold has put all life to sleep
Within the pond.
Only this strange ice creature—
Hollow-eyed, with nostrils wide—
In one long, desperate embrace
Triumphs your peak
To hold in trust for glacial time
The secrets of your frozen pyramid.

—*Shulamith Levey Oppenheim*

Ice Cycle

I've always thought it rather nice
That water freezes into ice.
I'm also pleased that it is true
That ice melts back to water, too.
But even so I find it strange
The way that ice and water change
And how a single water drop
Can fathom when it's time to stop
Its downward drip and go ahead
And start an icicle instead.

—*Mary Ann Hoberman*

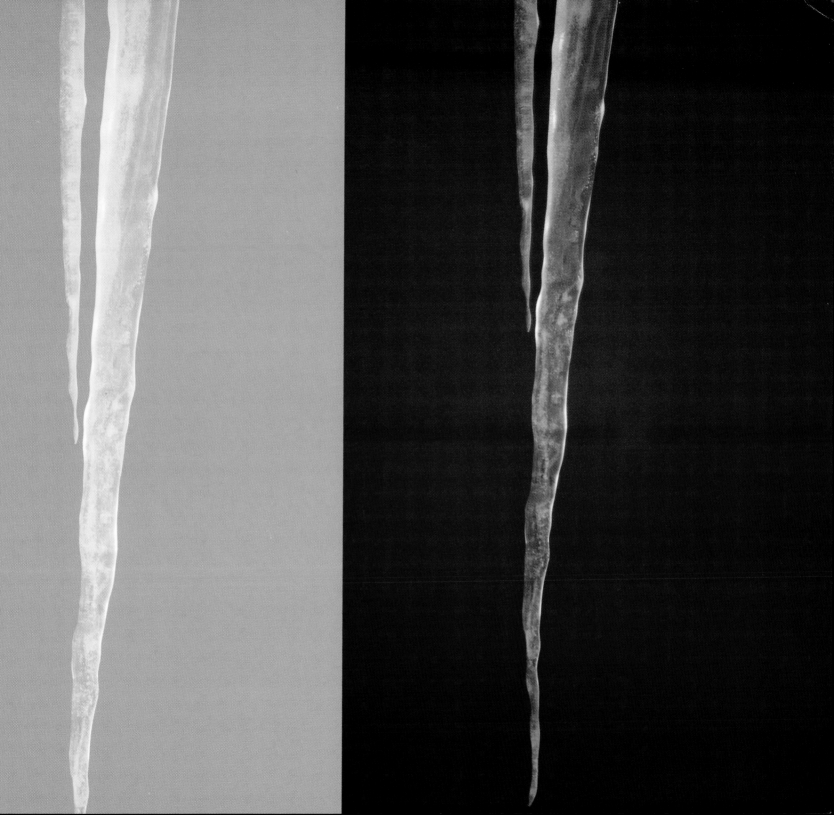

My Dog,

My Rough
Champion

Sit!—on the snowbank there beyond
This frozen windowpane of pond,
And tell me, Niño, how you draw
Such beautiful designs by paw.
I saw you take that headlong start—
Is this a dog's idea of art?
A Labrador retriever's show
Of Japanese haiku in snow?
Headline: **CHAMPION MAKES HIS MARK!**
They'll call it *Blues in Central Park*.
Artist: Niño,
Canvas: Ice,
Landscape: New York paradise.

—*J. Patrick Lewis*

24

Hieroglyph

A slip, a slide
of feathered toe
and furry leg
that brush the ice
and leave a message
for all to read:
one weasel, here,
before sunup,
dancing in the moonshine
snow.

—*Ann Turner*

Cold Snap

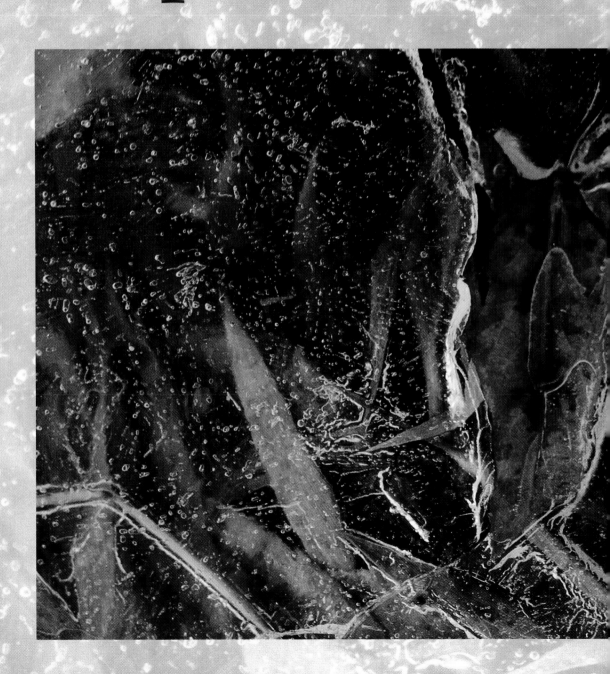

Fall cold
snaps closed
winter springs.

Winter springs
leave fall's
leaves frozen.

Winter spans
frozen falls,
frozen springs.

Falling forward,
spring snaps
winter open.

—*Bill Yake*

Once Upon Ice

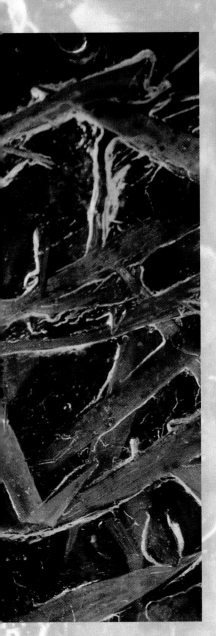

A tiny thing, dry, thin, and light,
just like a moth's abandoned wing,
and yet this frozen leaf's still bright,
singing the praises of the chance which lets it rest
forever now upon this glassy, frozen skin.
Had it fallen left or right,
it would have drowned or soon been swept
along the river like a raft
to that stone island and been wrecked—
or so a watcher might suppose tracing its imagined plight—
but here it beckons like a lighthouse,
tiny diary of itself, saved from disappearance yet,
and like Egyptian tombs of old
full of stories of the dead,
amasses wealth against the night.

—*Christine Crow*

28

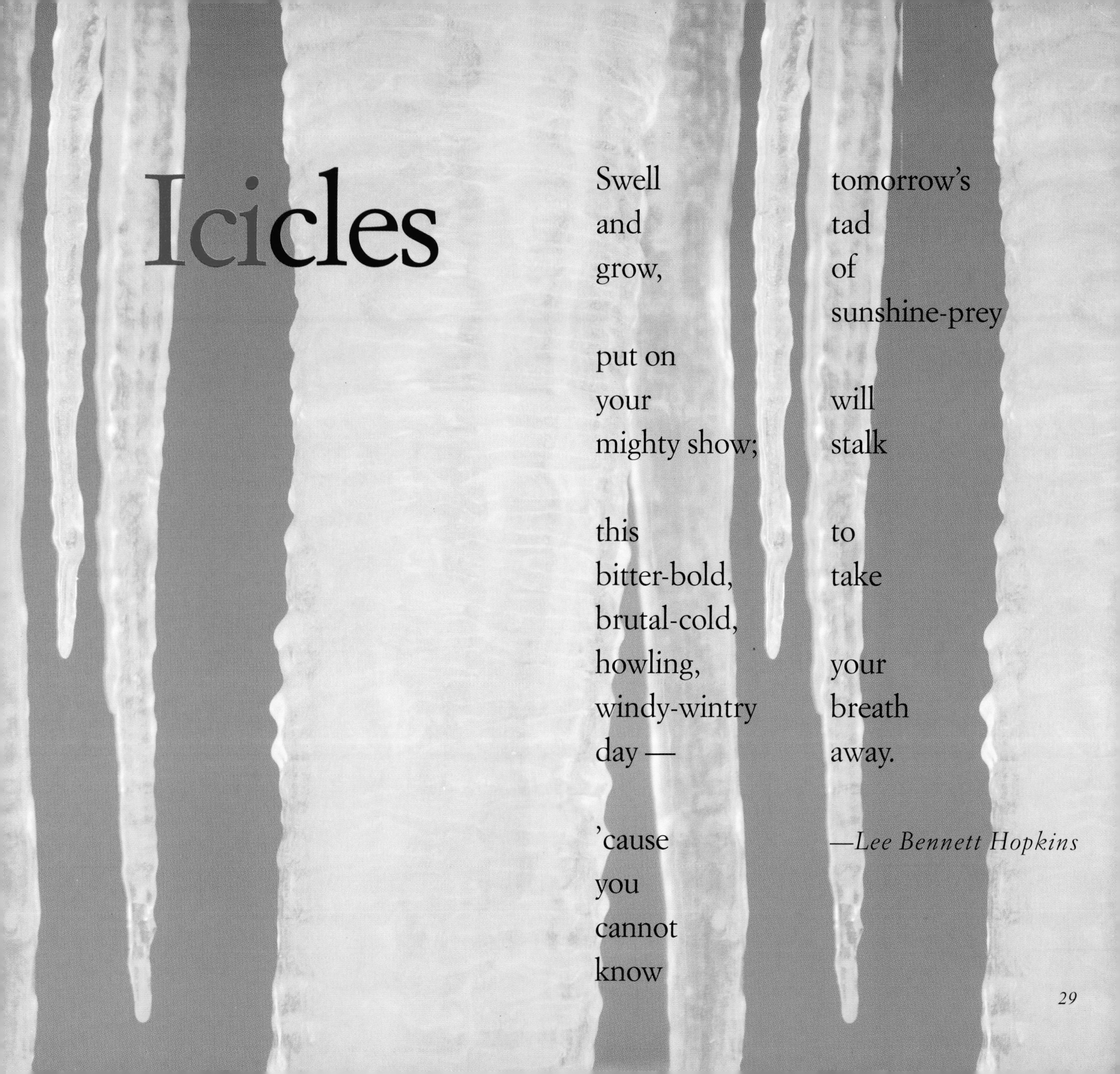

Icicles

Swell
and
grow,

put on
your
mighty show;

this
bitter-bold,
brutal-cold,
howling,
windy-wintry
day —

'cause
you
cannot
know

tomorrow's
tad
of
sunshine-prey

will
stalk

to
take
your
breath
away.

—Lee Bennett Hopkins

29

Ice Bridge

Imagine a billy goat
All a-shiver
Going across
This frozen river.

He uses the ice
For stepping stones
While frost intrudes
Into his bones.

Will he get far
Across the ice?
Or will he have
To pay the price

To some exacting
Winter troll
Who takes his life
To pay the toll?

—*Jane Yolen*

The Window in Winter

Who seeded this garden
of sapphires cut
to lettuce, opals

crushed to coral
cells for crabs, whelks,
fish finned in pearls,

lovely behind frost
caught in the act
of planting

a bed of rhubarb,
so radiant the sun
is already eating it?

—Nancy Willard

December Leaves

December leaves
  Behind sleet showers,
    A chilled bouquet
      Of azure flowers. . . .

Or should I call
  What winter turns
    From frost to glaze
      Blue window-burns?

—*J. Patrick Lewis*

Overnight Ice

Next time, this is what I'll remember
when I'm afraid: the ice on my window.

I'll remember how it filled up the glass
where there was nothing before,

where there was nothing, and I could see
clearly the full moon and stars. And then

while I slept, the ice came almost
like a snowflake, or a secret, spreading

in the cold, making itself up in the dark.
And this morning, it could be sugar

or the mane of a pony or a rooster's comb
that sticks my fingers to the window

glass. I'll remember this morning's ice.
It has the magic of the moon, bubbling.

—*Barbara Davis*

Proteus

When I was water you couldn't catch me,
though I filled the shape of a glass exactly.
When I was ice, my heart grew chill,
and I cracked the glass I was meant to fill.
Now I lie silent, hard and still,
and you *think* you can catch me.
No more than a rain cloud over the hill,
you never will, though.
Never will.

—*Christine Crow*

Ice Sisters

Fevered nights, we held the water bottle close
when chill and heat alternately shook us, the
windows outside coated with ice and the
patterns of feathers.

Well, we knew winter.
Water that bubbled up anywhere had to freeze,
and we laced up skates with silver blades and
flew across Spy Pond like birds.

Arms and legs and hair moving and the rushes
on the island and the sun going down.

Short days, so we skated into nights where
stars hung liquid and molten and the ice
boomed beneath us, cracking in long, sharp,
sudden cracks that startled us out of our
bright, gliding stupor.

Wind came up in the day sometimes, and we'd
stretch our arms, our coats, waiting for
wind's power to move us like the sailing ships
of old.

Put up your skysails, your star- and moonsails!
(we'd shout)

And we wanted to be the ice sometimes, lying
down on it, our eyes to the crystals,
formations, bubbles in that deep, inky black.

—*Pamela Powell*

Ice Cubes

Ice cubes
in a glass.
The sun comes
out.
Alas.
A loss
of form,
of firm-
ness
attributed
to warm-
ness.

—*Jane Yolen*

Acknowledgments

Every possible effort has been made to trace the ownership of each poem included in Once Upon Ice. If any errors or omissions have occurred, corrections will be made in subsequent printings, provided the publisher is notified of their existence.

Permission to reprint copyrighted poems is gratefully acknowledged to the following:

Kathi Appelt for "Chewing on Ice." Copyright © 1997 by Kathi Appelt.

Carol Jane Bangs for "Winter's Finger." Copyright © 1997 by Carol Jane Bangs.

Marvin Bell for "The Opera of the Ice." Copyright © 1997 by Marvin Bell.

Christine Crow for "Once Upon Ice" and "Proteus." Copyright © 1997 by Christine Crow.

Curtis Brown for "Icicles" by Lee Bennett Hopkins. Copyright © 1997 by Lee Bennett Hopkins; and for "Hieroglyph" by Ann Turner. Copyright © 1997 by Ann Turner; and for "Ice Bridge," "Ice Can Scream," "Ice Cubes," and "Necklace" by Jane Yolen. Copyright © 1997 by Jane Yolen. Printed by permission of Curtis Brown Ltd.

Barbara Davis for "Overnight Ice." Copyright © 1997 by Barbara Davis.

Ann Dixon for "Autumn." Copyright © 1997 by Ann Dixon.

Mary Ann Hoberman for "Ice Cycle." Copyright © 1997 by Mary Ann Hoberman.

X.J. Kennedy for "Dangerous Ice." Copyright © 1997 by X.J. Kennedy.

J. Patrick Lewis for "December Leaves" and "My Dog, My Rough Champion." Copyright © 1997 by J. Patrick Lewis.

Shulamith Levey Oppenheim for "Pyramid." Copyright © 1997 by Shulamith Levey Oppenheim.

Pamela Powell for "Ice Sisters." Copyright © 1997 by Pamela Powell.

Carol E. Reed-Jones for "Winter Wraps." Copyright © 1997 by Carol E. Reed-Jones.

Nancy Willard for "The Window in Winter." Copyright © 1997 by Nancy Willard.

Bill Yake for "Cold Snap." Copyright © 1997 by Bill Yake.